I0814978

KIDS ASK ABOUT

Written by Jocelyn Hubbell
Illustrated by Jean Cassels

Visit us at
SequoiaKidsMedia.com
for bonus
downloadable content

Photography © Shutterstock 2022 Michael Benard; Ryan M. Boltonv; Deatonphotos; W. de Vries; Michiel de Wit; Brian Lasenby; LittleCuckoo; Jennifer White Maxwell; Alyssa Metro; SAKDA NARATHIPWAN; Marius Neacsa; Jay Ondreicka; Javi Roces; Manfred Ruckszio; Annette Shaff; Carolina K. Smith MD; USBFCO

Published by Sequoia Kids Media,
an imprint of Sequoia Publishing & Media, LLC

Sequoia Publishing & Media, LLC,
a division of Phoenix International Publications, Inc.

8501 West Higgins Road, Chicago, Illinois 60631
34 Seymour Street, London W1H 7JE
Heimhuder Straße 81, 20148 Hamburg

Customer Service: CS@SequoiaKidsBooks.com

www.SequoiaKidsMedia.com

Library of Congress Control Number: 2022920284

ISBN: 979-8-7654-0173-6

KIDS ASK ABOUT

TABLE OF CONTENTS

WHO are frogs?

Frogs are amphibians (am-FIB-ee-enz). All amphibians are ectothermic—or cold-blooded—which means their body temperature is the same as the temperature around them. To warm up, frogs sunbathe in moist places where their skin will stay in top condition—wet and slimy!

IT'S A FACT!
The word "amphibian" comes from the Greek "amphibious," which means "living a double life." Most baby frogs live in the water and look nothing like the adults that live on land.
Green frog
DID YOU KNOW?
Most frogs have smooth, moist skin. They do not have feathers, fur, or scales.

HOW do frogs grow up?

Frogs' bodies undergo some astounding changes before they become adults. This is called metamorphosis (met-uh-MOR-foh-sis). It has three steps.

WHAT is the first step in frog metamorphosis?

Frogs begin their lives as soft, jelly-like eggs. Most adult female frogs lay their eggs in water. They place their eggs where the babies will be able to find food and hide from hungry predators such as birds, fish, and turtles.

DID YOU KNOW?
Some frogs lay just one egg while others lay 50,000 or more!
Spring peepers
WHERE do frogs lay their eggs?
Some frogs lay their eggs in damp areas on the ground among leaves or mosses. Others make foamy nests in trees or on the ground. A few types of frogs carry their eggs with them until they hatch.

WHAT is the second step in frog metamorphosis?

After several days to several weeks, larvae hatch from the eggs. Larvae are also called tadpoles. They have large, round heads and long, slender tails for quick swimming. They breathe underwater with gills just like fish.

Tadpoles

WHAT do tadpoles eat?

Most tadpoles are herbivores, or plant eaters. They filter out small particles of plant material in the water or scrape at vegetation with their tiny teeth. Some tadpoles are carnivores, or meat eaters. They eat tiny insects, animals, and other frogs' eggs!

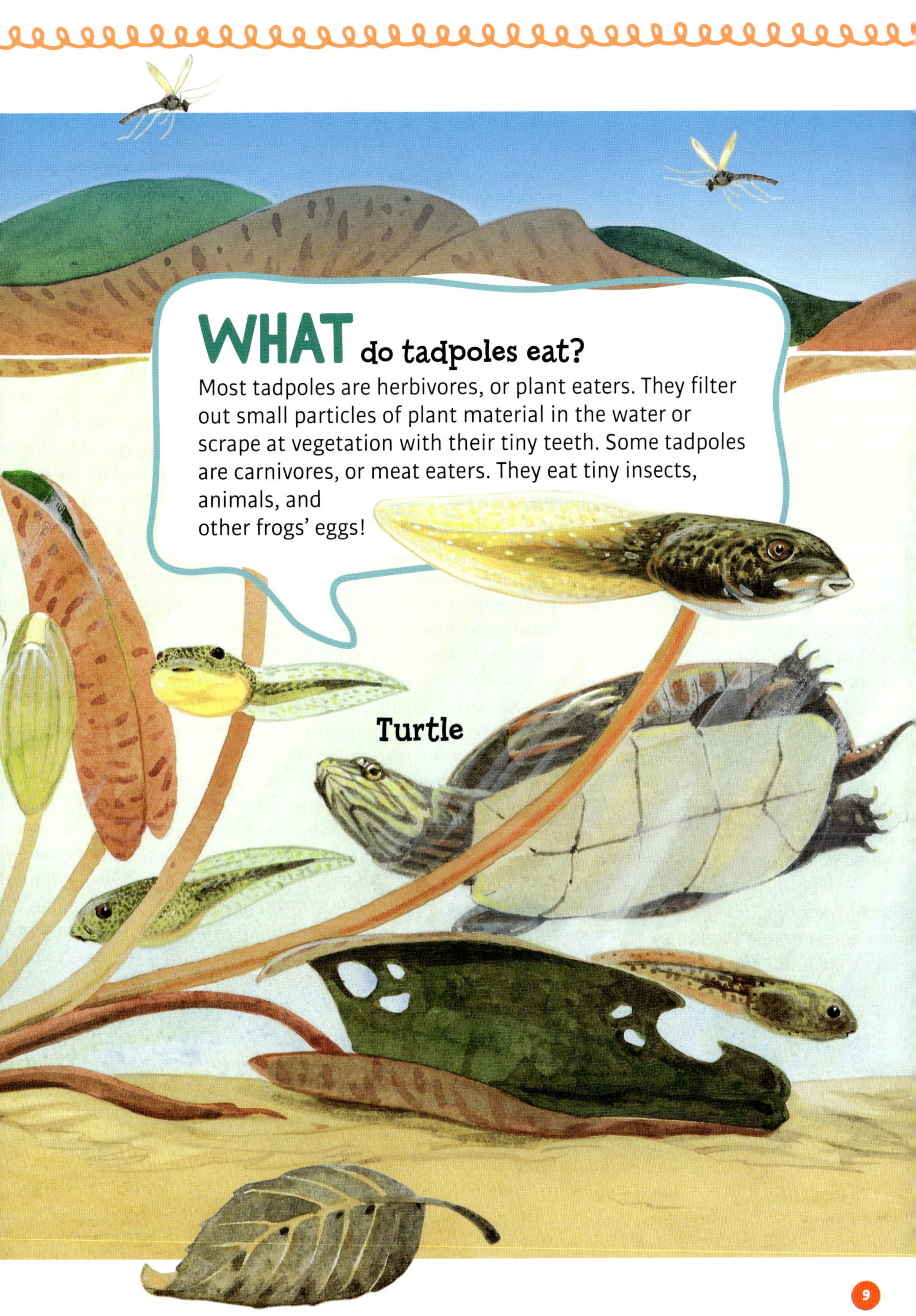

HOW do tadpoles change as they grow?

As tadpoles grow, internal gills take the place of their external gills. Within a few months they grow hind legs, then front legs. Their tails slowly shorten. Then their eyes and mouths become larger. Tadpoles also begin to grow lungs. They swim to the water's surface to test their lungs by gulping air.

DID YOU KNOW?

Some frogs do not have a tadpole stage. They hatch from eggs as tiny froglets.

WHAT is the third step in frog metamorphosis?

After two to four months, most tadpoles are ready to become adult frogs. The adults no longer have gills. Like you, they use lungs to breathe. Using long, powerful hind legs and webbed feet, the adults can now walk, hop, or jump on land, and swim in water. There are even frogs that can climb trees.

DID YOU KNOW?
Some frogs remain tadpoles for a long time. A bullfrog may be a tadpole for up to two years.
Gray treefrog
FROG METAMORPHOSIS
Egg
Tadpole
Hind legs appear
Front legs appear
Adult

WHY are frogs so slimy?

Some frogs have special glands in their skin that produce mucus—that's the stuff that makes frogs feel slimy! Others produce a waxy substance to keep their bodies from losing water and drying out. Frogs will die if they don't keep their skin moist.

American bullfrog

DID YOU KNOW?

Treefrogs have sticky mucous glands on their toes that help them climb.

Gray treefrog

DID YOU KNOW?

Believe it or not, scientists have developed many life-saving medicines from the chemicals in frogs' skin!

IT'S A FACT!

As frogs grow, they have to shed their skin. This is called molting. When molting, the old skin splits down the back. Then the frog uses its hind legs to push the skin over its head and into its mouth—then eats it!

HOW do frogs use their eyes?

A frog can see in all directions with its bulging, high-set eyes. They see things best from a distance of 2 to 20 feet (0.6–6 meters) away. Up close, a fly could hide right in front of a frog's nose! Frogs' eyes do more than just see. They also help a frog swallow its food! When a frog has taken in a large mouthful, it pulls its eyes into the roof of its mouth to help push the food down its throat.

IT'S A FACT!
Frogs' ears are called tympanums (tim-PA-numz). Frogs can hear very well.
American bullfrog
Tympanums
DID YOU KNOW?
Many frogs use their sense of smell to guide them back to the ponds where they were born to lay their own eggs.

WHAT do frogs eat?

Most frogs hunt at night and eat insects. Many of them also eat spiders, snails, slugs, worms, crayfish, and other small animals.

Northern leopard frog

DID YOU KNOW?

One frog can eat up to 10,000 insects in one summer!

HOW do frogs eat?

Most frogs have big mouths and long, sticky tongues. They flick out their tongues to catch prey. Frogs have small, sharp teeth that tightly hold prey so it cannot escape as it is being swallowed whole! They catch larger prey with their mouth or front feet.

IT'S A FACT!

Chilean helmeted bullfrogs eat insects, birds, fish, mice, snakes, small turtles, and even other frogs.

Chilean helmeted bullfrog

WHAT is the difference between frogs and toads?

Actually, all toads are frogs—but not all frogs are toads! Toads are a subclassification of frogs. Toads share certain physical characteristics with frogs and also have some unique ones of their own.

FROGS

Southern leopard frog

IT'S A FACT!

A group of frogs is called an army, while a group of toads is called a knot.

TOADS

American toad

DID YOU KNOW?

Frogs have to be able to hide or run from predators. They must also survive extreme temperatures and periods without food.

Poison dart frogs are brightly colored to warn predators that they are poisonous.

African bullfrogs can give predators sharp, painful bites!

Wood frogs and gray treefrogs can survive the winter because their bodies produce a natural antifreeze!

Flying frogs can leap out of trees and glide using their large webbed feet as parachutes.

Some frogs puff up their bodies to look bigger when facing a predator.

Many frogs dig into the ground to escape long periods of heat and dryness. Other frogs may sleep through winter buried in mud at the bottom of a pond until spring.

FROGS ARE AMAZING!
They live on all the continents except Antarctica, and they've been around since the time of the dinosaurs. Most frogs live near ponds, lakes, and swamps—but not all of them. Some live in deserts, others in jungles and the cold Arctic—you may even find these amazing amphibians...
...IN YOUR OWN BACK YARD!

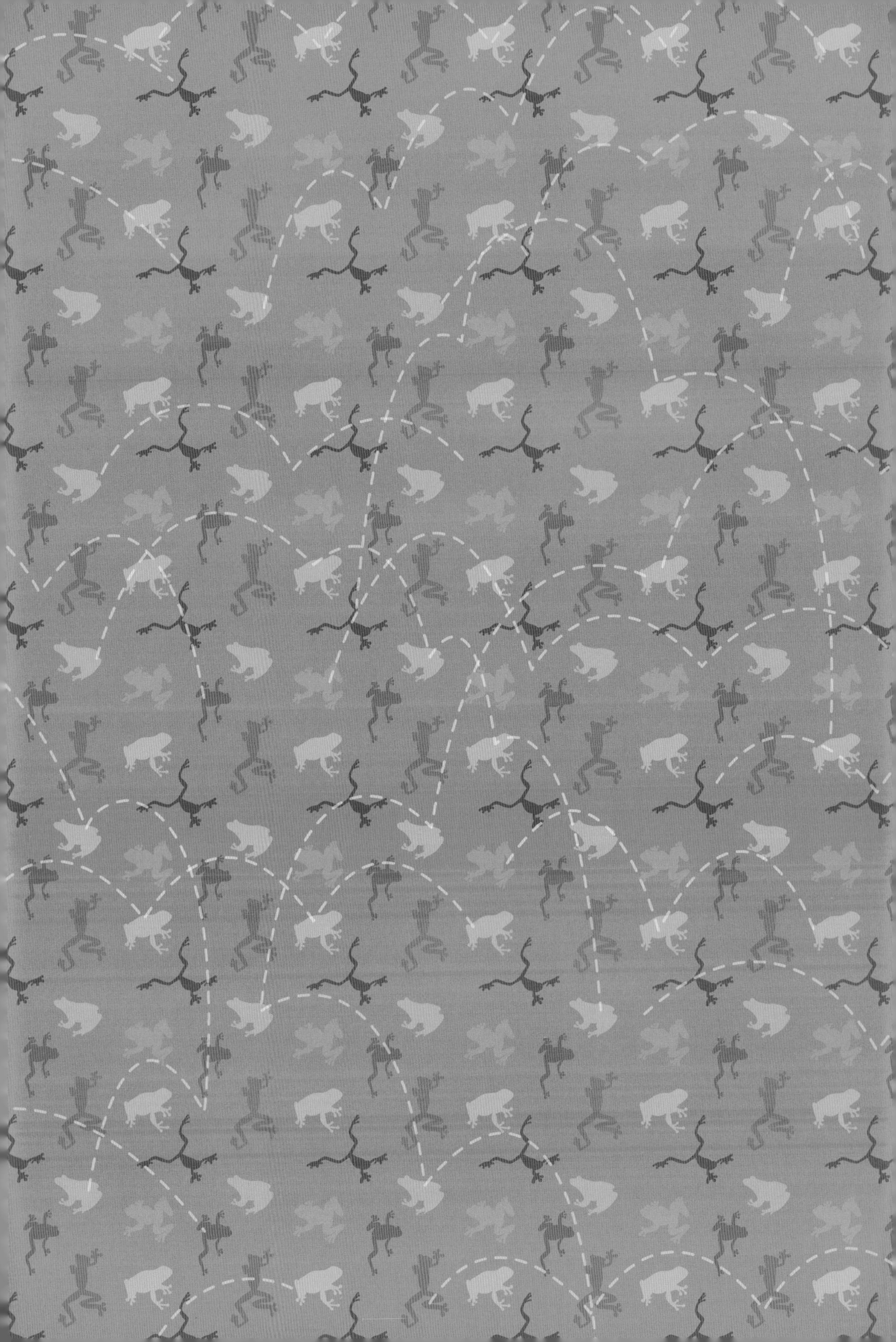